# 100 Loving Thoughts To My Children

*Life lessons and ideas for joy and success*

Choose love !

Sherry

## Sherry Ramrattan Smith

AuthorHouse™
1663 Liberty Drive
Bloomington, IN 47403
www.authorhouse.com
Phone: 1-800-839-8640

Published by AuthorHouse  03/15/2013

ISBN:  978-1-4817-1641-3 (sc)

Library of Congress Control Number: 2013903317

authorHOUSE®

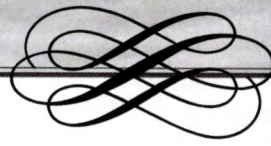

For my beautiful sons Ben and Matt

As the years pass, you will discover your own life lessons. I write these ideas and suggestions as gifts of my support and love. Modify them as you see fit. Use your creativity and imagination to connect them to your endeavours.

Always know that you are loved. Love brought you into this world and love will take you through life's journeys.

Share your love. Make your choices based on love, not fear. Such choices will let others know that you are lovable. Being a loving and caring person will lead you to a wider circle of love.

Accept and be grateful for each gift you receive. The act of giving demonstrates care and thoughtfulness. Receive graciously.

When someone does something nice for you, be sure to express your appreciation. Write a note or send an email. Let the person know that you value their time, gift, or gesture of goodwill.

Take time everyday to be alone. You only need a few minutes. Take a walk, exercise, play music, or sit quietly. Your brain and body will thank you for it and everyone else will benefit from the results.

Make a list of ten things you enjoy. Try to do at least three of them each week. It is best if the things you choose do not cost money, but if they do, then set aside a little bit of cash from each paycheck for them.

**F**orgive yourself for mistakes. Think about how things could be improved and make a plan for another try.

**S**miles are free. Share them often and not only with people you know.

**W**hen things do not go well, reflect, *dust-off*, and try again with a new perspective.

**S**tart each day with a positive thought. It can be something you want to accomplish or something you wish for someone you love.

**B**e appreciative of the beauty of nature. Hold on to the energy of lakes, mountains, oceans, forests, flowers, wildlife, and rainbows.

**E**at an apple or a piece of fruit you enjoy. Take time to savour its flavour.

**B**eautify a place in your home. It can be a corner or a room. Make it your special place by adding colours you like or items that hold personal meaning. Spend a few minutes each day in your place.

**D**onate items you do not require or use. As time goes by, our needs and likes change. Sometimes it becomes necessary to give away items in order to move to a new stage of life. Take a photograph and write a note to remember the significance of particular items.

Stare at the moon. The moon is magical and radiant beams of moonlight can help you to put your life into perspective. As you look at the moon, think about its beauty and your purpose as a capable and loving person.

After you read a book, consider sharing it with a friend or donating it to a library so that others can read it too.

Write down as many stories of your life as you can. Your life experiences can help others and more importantly you can begin to delve more deeply into the meaning of your experiences as you reflect upon them.

Say goodnight to everyone in your house, including your pets.

When you wake up, say good morning to everyone in your household, including your pets.

Collect all your change each day. Use a big jar or bowl. Never leave money lying around on the floor or on counters. Money is valuable. Remember some people do not even have a dime to spare. Put your money to good use.

Brush and floss as often as you can, every day. You will have a great smile and better health.

Find the best, most courteous hair stylist you can afford. A great haircut can do wonders for your self-esteem and confidence.

Exercise each day. If you can, go for a walk. If you can afford it, buy yourself an elliptical machine, a treadmill, and some weights. You need to be in good health in order to carry out your responsibilities.

Take plenty of photographs. Pictures mark our journeys and document our histories. Use them in scrapbooks or create a slide show to share at family gatherings.

Turn off your blackberry or cell phone in order to rest. The world will still go on and you will be able to catch up once you have had a break.

If you are able, donate some money to a different charity from every paycheck. There are many good causes that deserve attention and can function more effectively with financial support. Share the research and responsibilities of selecting charitable organizations with family members.

Buy two of the best glasses you can afford and drink two glasses of water as soon as you wake up. Keep one glass at work and one at home. Keep them filled with water and take sips frequently throughout the day. Water is one of the simple gifts of life. It connects us to the lakes, rivers, and oceans, the rain, and our tears. Every living thing needs water.

Read books that are inspiring. Whether a story is about someone who has faced a particular challenge and worked to overcome it, or tips to become a more effective listener, you can benefit from lessons that others have to share.

Say no to illicit drugs and if you drink alcohol, then learn to consume it in moderation. Such substances can be addictive and not only impair your thought processes and actions but may also cause financial stress.

Wake up early and watch the dawn. Seeing the beginning of a new day can precipitate positive changes. Watching the daybreak can help you to realize that you are a significant part of something much larger.

Play or listen to music every day. Music can restore the soul, connect you to memories, and change your mood. Writing, creating, and playing music are gifts that are to be shared.

If your work and living circumstances permit, then get yourself a pet. Pets love you unconditionally. They can help you to hone the skills and responsibilities of being kind and loving.

Learn to say no to extra work or unnecessary social invitations gracefully. For work, it is not wise to over-extend yourself. There are other matters that are just as important and deserve your attention. Regarding social invitations, ask yourself: How important is this occasion to me? Do I enjoy the person's company? Would I benefit more (mentally and physically) by attending or turning it down at this time?

Listen to your heart. Sometimes when we have tough decisions to make, we become overly dependent on logic and rational thought to guide us. But deep inside, there can be a *feeling* that interrupts or counteracts the logic. Pay attention to that feeling. That is the wisdom of your own voice. It may be warning you of risks that need to be addressed or steering you towards a more suitable goal.

Find time to rest each day. Whether it is a ten-minute power nap, snoozing while watching television, or a good night's sleep, resting provides a way to re-energize your body and mind.

Make time for play. Playing is healthy. Throw a ball to the dog, build a campsite in the living room with your children, or do a puzzle. Engaging in an activity that is fun or relaxing can shift your focus from deadlines and can make you more productive when you return to work.

Be purposeful and loving in your conversations. Time flies by so use it wisely to listen and to share your ideas. Advice is not always welcomed ☺. Instead, offer suggestions and some of the lessons you have learned through your experiences.

Think of yourself as full and complete. No one needs to *complete* you. You can share your life and experiences with others in meaningful ways that can bring you joy but you have everything that is necessary within you to lead a happy life.

**R**eadily acknowledge meaningful relationships in your life. Let people know that you appreciate them for their kindness, love, and trust.

**G**o for joy! To experience joy, you need to take time to value all the blessings in your life. Whether it is celebrating an academic accomplishment or taking a walk with your partner, stop and savour the moments by being fully present.

**D**o as much as you can to learn about yourself. As you gain insight into your thoughts and actions, you also become more aware of everyone else around you – their needs and wants.

**F**ocus attention on what you want to accomplish. Set specific goals and actions. Expend the necessary effort to move towards what you are aiming for. Small steps do matter.

**L**augh at yourself. We all do ridiculous things. When you find yourself making a mountain out of a molehill, find the humour of the situation. Tell yourself: *I am in a funny place!*

Simplify your routines. Whether it is breakfast, exercise, or bedtime, streamline your routines by organizing them into three easy steps. This may also help your children learn to establish their own routines faster.

If you have an assignment, double the estimated time to complete it. If you happen to finish early, use the time to get some feedback that can help to make it even better.

Give yourself time to think. Sifting through ideas or creating new ones comes from thought. As you spend time with your ideas, you will be better able to put your attention where it is most needed.

**B**e generous with your love, laughter, and talents.

**L**earn to reinvent yourself when necessary. Select the very best parts of who you are and carry them forward. Try to incorporate new qualities that you admire in others.

**S**trive for justice and speak out against injustices. Use your conscience as a guide to determine what actions are right and wrong. This type of *moral compass* will help you to choose to do the right thing, even when it may not be the most popular choice.

17

**E**mulate qualities of people you admire. Ask yourself, why do I like these individuals?

**A**ctions matter. Choose your actions carefully and after due consideration.

**I**t is perfectly okay to be emotional. Our feelings connect us to our values. Become comfortable with the expression of your emotions and learn to articulate why you carry such strong feelings.

**F**ocus on what matters. Life if full of trivialities that can keep you occupied and running in circles. Ask yourself, how will this matter a week from now or a year from now?

**L**earn the difference between knowledge and wisdom. Your wisdom will grow as you build and apply your knowledge.

18

Contribute in meaningful ways. Whether it is participating in a food drive, writing a blog, or volunteering to drive children home after a game, find a way to be of service to your community.

Understand the wonders of living with confidence. Confidence comes from building awareness of yourself – your strengths and weaknesses, likes and dislikes, beliefs and values. Confident people use their knowledge and conscience to guide their decisions.

Focus on the best attributes in the people you meet. To do this requires deep listening and looking beyond surface glossiness or inadvertent mistakes. Think instead about what is great or intriguing about a person.

Learn something new every day. Think of yourself as a life-long learner.

Try and try again until you succeed. If you believe that you want to accomplish a goal, then plod away at it. It could take a while, but persist. It is possible to achieve it. Sometimes the pathway is not always straight so be prepared to follow the curves.

Anticipate the outcomes you desire. Daydream about them when you can. Our dreams can ignite our passions and lead us to take practical steps toward our goals.

Live your passion. Listen to your heart to find out what makes you excited and happy. Then take a small step. You will know if it is right if you feel a sense of joy and accomplishment. If you feel heavy and worried, then you will know the step you took may not be one that is right for you. So, plan another different step and take it.

Live your life with zest. Raise the bar each day to achieve the life you want to live.

Make a long-term commitment to get to know yourself. It takes courage to examine ourselves. You will come face-to-face with your strengths, weaknesses, or gaps in your knowledge. As you learn about yourself and take steps to improve, the better equipped you will be to understand your relationships.

Know your community. Community networks can provide information and support.

In new situations, inquire and learn to maintain a stance of curiosity. Think: *I want to see how this will turn out.*

Talk to other people. Our histories, experiences, and identities matter. Knowledge and meaning are collective productions and require testing our interpretations of situations with others. Keep in mind that we speak to one another from different socio-cultural and political contexts. Aspects of our identities will play out.

Remember that we understand one another based on what we carry: differences in experiences, privilege, labels, visible and invisible markers. When you enter into conversations with a goal to improve relationships, you have to be willing to hear critique and acknowledge different perspectives.

Pay attention to contexts. It is crucial to bring a critical lens to interactions and experiences. Living is not done on a level playing field. Some people have more access and hold more power than others.

**B**ecome more mindful of assumptions you make and unintentional messages you send by your actions or inactions. Be aware.

**R**ead widely and try to keep up with best practices and current research ideas. Try them out and see what works best with your goals.

**B**ecome a critical consumer of information. Learn to sort through what you read, see, and hear to make the best decision.

**C**heck your options. When choices have to be made, go through the possible outcomes. Then select accordingly.

**T**hink ahead. Life happens. Thinking and planning ahead will help you overcome obstacles easier and will prevent muddling through.

**H**old yourself responsible for your actions. Blaming others is easy to do. However, if you are accountable to yourself you will grow your determination to succeed. Your confidence and decision-making abilities will also improve.

**B**e an optimist. Looking on the bright side will get you over there faster than wallowing in self-pity.

**A**ccept the fact that there are joys and disappointments in life. Keep moving forward.

**R**emember that you are never too young or too old to learn something new or think about things from another perspective. Remain open-minded.

**A**pologize when you are wrong.

**A**void blaming others.

**S**hop from your own closet first before you buy something new.

**E**at healthy foods.

**W**atch funny shows and read humorous stories. We all benefit from laughter.

**K**eep a record of how you spend your money. Check to see how your expenditures match your goals and what you say you value. Are you spending your money on what you consider as important?

**F**orgive, forgive, and forgive. Never mind, just let it go.

**A**sk for assistance when you need it. We can all benefit from help.

**B**ecome an activist. Learn about how simple actions such as signing petitions, canvassing, and participating in boycotts can shape the future for the better.

**S**top and take notice of snapshots of your life. What has improved? What needs attention?

**N**ote your opinions, likes, and dislikes. How have they evolved over time?

**E**mbrace your history. Come to terms with it. Use a scrapbook, album, or data file to trace as much of your background as you can. Knowing about your family's struggles and accomplishments can help you appreciate where you are in your journey and provide guideposts.

When you feel the world bearing down on your shoulders, play or listen to as many songs as you can about feeling free. Here are my suggestions: *Free as a bird, Born Free, I'm Like a Bird, Rock Steady,* Theme from *A Summer Place.*

Make everyday moments - marvellous ones. Take time to feel the warmth of the sun on your skin, wind in your hair, rain on your face, and snow melting in your hands.

Find fulfillment through service to others. Share your talents, teach someone to read, volunteer to lend a hand in a community beautification project, or take the lead in organizing a charitable event.

Choose to change. Embark on simple ways to improve how you live your life. Whether it be clearing clutter or taking a course, small steps can lead to positive results.

Create a memory box. Select about a dozen items that are meaningful. Write a few sentences about each one. Share your memories with friends and family at opportune moments.

Take time to appreciate the unexpected – today I saw three deer hop a fence to enjoy the neighbour's rose bushes. What spectacular sights are you missing?

Organize your home so that there is a place for everything. This will save you a lot of time and frustration.

**A**llow new opportunities to unfold. Observe, wait, and observe some more. Avoid jumping to conclusions or making hasty decisions.

**T**ry a *change experience* experiment every year. Pick one thing you would like to improve upon and try it out for at least 21 days. Write about your experience.

**R**ead or listen to something to build your knowledge every day. Then find ways to share what you have learned. It is your turn to help to pave the way for others by your choices and actions.

**F**orge your own traditions. Think of your life as though it is a legacy – an enchanting musical composition, a poem to contemplate upon, or a mesmerizing painting. Make it the best it can be.

*...I wish you joy and success in your endeavours...with love*

## A Considerate Curriculum

A considerate curriculum is a viable way to engage school and community in taking up our differences, similarities, practices, and actions with an aim to improve our understanding of one another. Emphasis is placed on our choices and actions. Conceptually, this way of thinking creatively "opens up" the joys of learning and teaching to everyone. Curriculum is not limited to the work of teachers, educational workers, and students. Instead, curriculum is situated in our daily interactions – within schools, among colleagues, friends, and families, and extends to our responsibilities as community members and global citizens.

*...Critical Connections: Teachers writing for social justice*

CPSIA information can be obtained
at www.ICGtesting.com
Printed in the USA
LVIW020902270313
326080LV00001BA